C.G. Dahlin was born in Decatur, Illinois and raised in Andover, Minnesota. He's recently graduated from the University of Wisconsin–Stout with a degree in Professional Communication and Emerging Media. During his studies, he was published by *Prometheus*, *Forward*, and *Pepper Magazine*. He's now working as a Researcher and English Tutor in Menomonie, Wisconsin.

Un/Certainly Form/Less

A Collection of
Grisingistic
Poetry

created and published by

C.G. Dahlin

2016

First Printing: 2016
978-0-692-69734-4

C.G. Dahlin
www.cgdahlin.com
dahlincg@gmail.com
@dahlincg

Acknowledgements:

Λευτέρης Αντάκης
&
UW–Stout Faculty, most notably:
Daniel Ruefman
Mitchell Ogden

Contents

Preface

In December of 2013, I was living meagerly within a cramped studio apartment in Aghia Paraskevi, Greece. I'd been recently inspired by the words of the Greek Philosopher-Poet, Λευτέρης Αντάκης (Lefteris Antakis). This marked the first time I'd written poetry on my own accord.

When I returned to the States, the University of Wisconsin–Stout's Honor's College incentivized me to continue writing. Now, being early May of 2016, this book has become a result of my work and research with both the Honor's College and the Digital Humanities Capstone Committee.

The aim of this collection is to reintegrate our use of form within poetics. As the history of this study shows, how we choose to form our poetic expression is a representation of our changing form within the modern day. In short, our changing form changes our form.

The onset of computerized mediums has sent poetry into a diversified state. Now that our written work can be enhanced by technological animation and augmentation, where does this leave print? What good is this static medium versus the capabilities of our increasingly engaging computers?

The proposed, Grisingism, takes on three initiatives. **(1) To experiment with the potentiality of the print medium**. If we, as poets, aren't using the kinetic and audio-enabled computerized mediums to enhance the engagement of our expression, then we ought to test the bounds of our age-old static print in ways that we never have before. With this critique considered, I've acted to justify the use of such a medium. Technology won't kill print, it's bound to change it and complement it in new ways.

(2) To allow the poetry to be overly abstract, abysmal, and ambiguous. Filtering a muse for readability is a tedious act. One that somewhere along the line strips it of its genuine nature and turns the words hollow, lacking of the immeasurable authenticity of the initial expression. The same fault can be committed once comparing a poet's individual work with those before him. Originality is hungered for but so often unrecognized by forced associations. This isn't to say that this process doesn't include its share of nonsense. This particular work recognizes that the true nature of things and poetry by extension, is at the middle of the scales, within an indistinguishable grey. A Grisingistic Collection therefore is a singing of the grey; making a Grisingistic Poet a grey-singer.

(3) To regard expression above coherence and incoherence. Narrative in this respect is certainly not a requirement. This form of expression can yet again act against the intention of a Grisingistic Poet. Each poem's intentionality, whether conscious or unconscious, remains paramount. This rigid individuality should not carry obligations to obey the conventions previously established by the poet themselves or the poets of the past and present. If a poem is presented in a traditional form, the question then becomes, why? Ought the form of the poem in some way resemble the underlying themes established by the content? If so, then the form ought to become a medium and be used to further the multifaceted expression of the poet.

Dear Philosophy,

Look at yourself fool!
You claim to know
why time travels
and why we watch it so.

You must be denser
than a singularity.
Why be so immovable
in such a shapeless grand scheme?

You stand in defiance;
The ultimate rejection
of the eternal flux.
A valiant feat indeed.

But even the trees,
with roots grasping the deep,
sway with the wind's passing.

Love,

Poetry

Part 1:
The Surface

To be
constrained
within a body that
decides it own
form.The
ugliness
or beauty bestowed.
By who? **Heaven** knows.
This noble vessel acts,
brings the world to be, decides
how I'm treated and how
I go about. Each little mole,
could be constellations mapped
upon the skin.
But who is to say?
A soul, within a valet.
What can be gathered
from such a figure?
A vision, from a
particular fission.
What can be **gathered**
from this? **The world**
is what the eyes miss.

Unable, Yet Fully

Deep feelings,
given word to,
forms not the feeling,

        but something new entirely.

Words aren't
sufficient for
understanding.
It requires more.
A type of intimacy,
a type of [u n s p o k e n] word.

[[[[These pulsing pressures of confusion,
these deliberating tethers of indecision,
offer me little except a mounting intensity.

I become restless,
take to the descending industrial straightaway,
feel the [u n s e e n] content of motion's passing
force upon my voluntary vessel.
Given words cycle through the raw neurons
of my sore and seizing cerebral meat.
Overflowing with electrical fluid data,
I'm still without the [u n s p o k e n] word.

Malnourished human appeals
leave me with piercing punctures
in (the constraints of the cage
that is) my ribs.]]]]

Can't find solace among given words,
can't illustrate my sharp impasse,
can't take in anymore.
This is the life I asked for.

Masks of Belonging Smiles

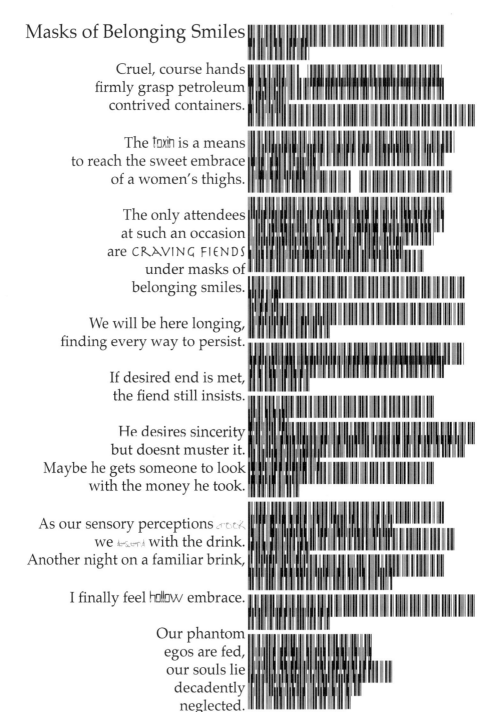

Cruel, course hands
firmly grasp petroleum
contrived containers.

The toxin is a means
to reach the sweet embrace
of a women's thighs.

The only attendees
at such an occasion
are CRAVING FIENDS
under masks of
belonging smiles.

We will be here longing,
finding every way to persist.

If desired end is met,
the fiend still insists.

He desires sincerity
but doesnt muster it.
Maybe he gets someone to look
with the money he took.

As our sensory perceptions crock
we descend with the drink.
Another night on a familiar brink,

I finally feel hollow embrace.

Our phantom
egos are fed,
our souls lie
decadently
neglected.

What Men Must Do

Vanished within the remnant shadings,
light's insistent glare faired not well
where he doggedly dwelled.

Latching to mental means.
       Graciously   imprisoned   and
perpetually propelled to
postponed ——————————————————————— purpose.

A boy,
who looked through
piercing eyes of torch flame blue,

came to the shade of the man.

Scoffed at, turned away.
What   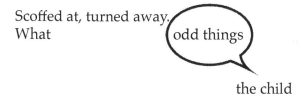

                    the child
                        will so naively say.

He's without the
[forgotten] lightness,
dense dichotomies weighing

                            foot to ground.

Let the child's *words* be regarded,
as mere sound.

Drooping Dreams

We'll argue about the blooms,
and neglect the
parched, contorting roots.

Good tidings come with subtle knowing of
forming, inevitable glooms.

To feed a forever dying subject,
to dwindle within the dreams
of our passionate [comm]+[union].
Ice stifling already fading flame.

When initiated, we knew
that such discrepancies
would come to mind's eye.
We knew that our intents
would never easily over
lie.

What misplaced quarrel
takes you from my grasp?
What DISTINCTION doesn't meet
your rigid vision?

The seed is not meant for this soil.
The strength of its growth
serves as nothing more
than a fallacious judgment,
a sickly bloom.

Yesterday's Tomorrow

A
day
like
today,
A day like
today, A day
like today, A
day like today,
A day like today,
A day like today,
A day like today, A
day like today, A
day like today, A
day like today, A
day like today,
A day like
today, A day
like today,
A day
like

On a day like today,
I don't feel like fighting
the insistent, inconsistent
dilemmas of the *hearsay*.
On a day like today,
I see that the drama,
the dream,
is as vast across
as the **asphalt roads**,
men tread on their way.
On a day like today,
I understand how all
the days that pass are as
I watch it, here [[[now]]].
I tell a sensible man
only to hear him say,
"It may."

A
day
like
today,
A day like
today, A day
like today, A
day like today,
A day like today,
A day like today,
A day like today, A
day like today, A
day like today, A
day like today, A
day like today,
A day like
today, A day
like today,
A day
like

It may.
In the demanding confines of seriousness
I stand, I no longer *dream* nor *play*.
Don't fool yourself longer.
See the **darkness** where
you choose to *stray*.
It may.
It is! I come to you
as kin, not by *distinct blood*
but by the very **blood within.**
Selflessly I say, to *yourself,* obey,
by not being a self
on a day like today.

It
may,
It may,
It may, It
may, It may,
It may, It may,
It may, It may, It
may, It may, It
may, It may,
It may, It
may, It
may,

It
may,
It may,
It may, It
may, It may,
It may, It may,
It may, It may, It
may, It may, It
may, It may,
It may, It
may, It
may,

Introversion

Tonight, leave me   alone.
I have put on the face
made of stone.
I wish for my own (   ) space.

The act tires me,
everyone forcing conversation.
I just want to be   alone,
in solemn meditation.

                                          Talk to me now,
                                          useless as ever.
Solitude

                                          is how
                              I heal from endeavor.

Chattering away,
whatever   one   can say,
                              to have the gathering
                              go their self-serving way.

                    I don't want to hear
              [empty] words spoken [clear].
                I want to hear [nothing]
              [no sound, not even mere…………………..........
....
....
....
....
....
....
....
....
....
....
....
....
....
....

Currently Real

/ Alongside the river's stream,
a writer jots down
a literary scheme.
He renders real things
as they seem.
little does he know
it could be but a dream. /

\ But things as they are
depend on how he deems
and how a particular mind
takes in what light beams.

From this,
reality really means
the real (is only hinted at
by just an) itty bit of it. \

/ Rest assured,
the cool river's flow
is as real as can be…

I mean, as real as the writer
and what he can see. \

Distant Relatives

The sky s   p   e   w   s .

                   .
                   s
                   t
                   u
                   o
                   r
The soil .   p
                   s

(The sky and the soil
bear no relational turmoil.)

The free one, *views.*

The cautious one doubts.

As if the world does not provide,
the purpose I seek,
the warmth of its withstanding hide.

No need to search for light to shed
we only fool ourselves,
the pleasures of being misled.

Find the answers if you decide,
within the living
and carried with all who have died.

(The soil and the sky
provides those with watchful eye.)

In the fall, we s   p   e   w   ,   ʹ
pass through, die.   t
                          u
                          o
                          r
                          p
The spring, we s
come to be, *by*

what relates [what crawls and what flies].

Who's Under the Skin

Walk here,   don't go there.
Be this,   don't be that.

Is it possible to be as you wish,
stand where you need,
and do so because that
would be you?

Maybe question your method
to see if it's true.
Because everyone
thinks they are,   yet nobody,   seems to be.

Who is it there,
that looks upon me
with scorching despise
that only can see

d   i   s   t   i   n   c   t   i   o   n   ?

Who are you
to tell me,
how to be?

Who is it that makes
your entrails churn,
what is it that has
your conditions yearn?

Surely it is I
who stands behind the veil,
but when covers lifted
there is no, one…
there is,
all
all
all
all   all
all
all
all   all   all   all

all   all   19   all

all

Part 2:
The Depths

We all hand each other
partial images. We masochistically
assume they've   misjudged me.
But you   were never
portrayed.   You   have   been hidden
behind   false   partial   images.
Your mask   has mended
into   your   face.
Take off   your fascade,
your starved   skin will be   rubbed raw
but   it will be   you.
You will   be   seen and
will feel   the burden
of such an uncommon image.
But at least this one
will be full;   will be the
person it   portrays.
Take off   your mask.
You'll never   see the one
you seek,   if they wear
the mask   as you do.
They will   never   recognize
you as the   love   they've
desired,   because   you
are   hidden,

never truly
seen by
anyone.

Endurance

The
early
morning
piercing gusts,
do nothing to stop
my straining muscles must's.
The ice seers my CRACKING face.
The elemental draughts may disintegrate
my mortal and forever changing flesh.
It doesn't batter my heart,
my consequential   n
yearning.   b   v
                                                                    i

          You may take me into   o
as long as what drives me to cast   o
[   ]out of confinements is retained   i
then this UNIVERSAL CONSTRUCT
will feel my sacred

                                                                    l

                    defiance.

In this way, I can be
the man who speaks of what is
because I can be he
who is no longer among us.
Human.

Consuming Cities

Watch where you step my darling.
These concrete slab streets are forged
to oppress the starved soil beneath them.

Tread on these avenues too long,
you'll find yourself lose
what makes you human.

!
          y
     l
F

Starved beneath a concrete slab.

Run now,
Never let these folly aims take.
The well-respected customs will drain you

slowly, as to not **ALARM** your senses.

You are *beauty*.
You are exactly as you should be,
but better.

Do not give this to the world.
You'll never see it in yourself again.

Keep it hidden.

There are few,
but some can still see,
the awe beyond the masks;

the true divinity.

For Somebody Somewhere

She asked me,
        "Where do you think you'll end up?"
And like with most questions,
I had to add just a pinch of sugar,
for a recipe that calls for at least a pound.
I said something like,
        "The sequoias of the
West call my name."
But really, I would leave those
bark behemoths
to turn even more bitter,
if only I knew
that I could construct a future
with you.

The wonders of this
gyrating geoid
mean less to my heart of hearts
than even the slightest glance,
past your admirable armor.

A life without love
is just an if;
and if I'm left to wonder forever [ever
I'll see my satisfaction come [never]...

So although you may not ever know
my true answer will always go,
        "Wherever you'll have me."

-ever -ev
-ever
-ever
-ever -ev
-ever -ever -ever -ever
-ever -ever -ever -ever
-ever -ever -ever -ever -ev
-ever -ever -ever
-ever

-ever

Broken Time

My alarm clock is broken.
It counts up to ten,
repeats over again.   now
It persists and sees time spoken.   now

Head in the sky,   now
I'm aloof with a perplexed mind.
Without tether, yet I'm still in bind,
                     ten seconds
          passes by.   now

I remain shy as to why   now
the clock counts as it does.   now
I realize that, now;
is always what it was.

                              now
One nor two nor three nor four.
Time is a stream, nothing more.
As to what second it is, no(w)-body-is sure.   now
                                                     now
As I meander,
without conscious gander,   now
          ten seconds
     pass.   now
This is recorded in frivolous gloss.

Can't you see
our constructions are smoke?
I realize this now because   now
my clock is broke.

I'll waste mine,   now
you'll spend yours.   now
There is no lineage line.
The now implores.

                              now
My alarm clock is broken.
It counts up to ten.
As the stream passes,
it counts over again.   now

Reintegration

Lollygagging until we're l i
Physicality perished.   m
The walking,   p
ascribe the purpose.   .
Those who are no longer aware
cannot bare [the c a r e] .

Live on, live on,
        all fall across the   s   t
                                      r
                                                            e
The winds of today are made
from former breaths,   t

[unseen]

        [unseen]

[unseen]   c
                        living days built up
                        by prior deaths.

    [unseen]   [unseen]   h

        [unseen][unseen]
[unseen]

[unseen]   [unseen]   The people of the past
                                whose names no longer ripple
            [unseen]   through the murky waters of time,
                        collectively compose the current's
[unseen]   [unseen]   confines.

                [unseen]   [unseen]

    [unseen]   [unseen]   The waters from the bedrock floors
                                         make their way up,
        [unseen]   the unseen always implores.
[unseen]   I'll be gone for however long,
                [unseen]   but you'll always hear my notes
[unseen]   [unseen]   [unseen]   in the ethereal song.

        [unseen]
                [unseen]

    [unseen]   [unseen]   25   [unseen]

Huge Leaps, No True Distance

Days, weeks, years,
implanted men since first hour,
sharpening spears.
Infused with clouded,
self-defining fears.
Victory, retribution,
in blood, the fooled cheers.

Raised to be [unful ed,   ]
from   end   to   end,
the earth mercilessly milled.
Striving, strife for elusive
purity instilled.
Endless Endless Endless Endless
Endless Endless Endless
obstacles, the people Endless
collectively willed. Endless Endless
Endless Endless
In the air's fairly
distributed malice, Endless Endless
innocence is made impossible by
society's glorified fucking phallus. Endless Endless
The rich lack wealth, Endless
sipping from empty promised chalice,
inner voids not filled, Endless
as the self proclaimed chosen Endless Endless
consequently contrive their dystopian palace. Endless Endless
Endless
Live, die, live, die; waxes and wanes, Endless Endless
[inner dilemma] illustrated by what's in the sky. Endless
Endless
As a mind,
as an embodiment of perceptiveness, Endless Endless
I can see eons pass, Endless
yet I still remain shy Endless Endless
as to the intend of the effort,
the biggest fear, the question, **why?**

In silent passing season, Endless Endless
man creates the problem Endless
and each serving reason. Endless
Endless
Endless

End

The Knower's Medium

No matter
what knowledge it is,
It's content is amorphous.
Any power that is given to it
solely depends on
how it's   (put, it's shaped,
                          it's brought about,
                    to what purpose it's)
formed.
Like the spaces b e t w e e n us,
                                    and the shadows behind us,

what can be known
is always [present   present   present   present   present

[Pages among pages,   ]
          novels upon novels,   present
          volumes following volumes,
          light years and eons across.

                                                        pre

It's known simply by the act
of choosing to know it,
                  (for value,
whether   for destiny,
                  for game of it,)
it is, just because it is [or not].

Let it be said,
let it be given hand,
that [nothing] is found
without (at least)
[unacknowledged] drive.

The whispers of your mind,
what ails you in the nights,
(and what has you rise in the mornings,)
is this very same shapelessness
that we form life out of.
This very same [nothing],
that we have made
[everything

everything everything
everything   everything everything   27
ything everything   everything   everything

Blurred Bliss

The pressing, cryptic mists
murmur wisdoms as they pass
through the gaps between the trees.

What brings such a forest
to sublime impressions?
Elemental nature proves to be...

                                       languid.

Although I am   d i s t i n g u i s h e d
from the air's collection,
I am shrouded in the ambiguity of it.

The stillness that ensues
from the blotching out of

what is seen,

restores any keen eye
to a state much like that before birth
and after we die.

This **space stealing** vapor,
this   forlorn fog,
has no place for those who have
certain trajectories.

I understand its [[[presence]]]
simply because,
I have no place to go.
I am so still,

                                    so secluded,

hidden   behind its veil.

What We Share

Our resonance

is the only thing felt
by the [[[[[Immortal's]]]]] passing glare.
Our tongue is not understood
by those of a separate sphere.

The meaning, the passion, the drive
is understood by all that fluxes.

The vigor of the flailing arms,
the fire behind despairing eyes

appeals to what moves the mountains,
what fills the skies.

Words, distinctive and unclear
are only heard by humanity's ear.
What **hardens** the rock
and *waves* the water,
feels those who carry
this inner glowing spectra,
this key to an *ethereal* Mecca.

So show meaning to what beats the heart,
what's been here with all end and start.
What has torn apart and *formed* together.
What allows me to see,
that whatever it is,
that we share,

will be here

forever [ever -ever

29

Abyssopelagic

Take what you will,

whatever of mine

that will finally fill
the depths of your design.

Reality-harsh,
satirical,

absurd.

The abyss speaks without word.
In all ways negates how
it ought to be.

Unbearable thirst quenched,
famished, hunger fed

A heart that will not
succumb:

The world ravishing and far
Feet overcome by encapsulating tar:

the fire not yet dead.

find your mind drenched
in further longings

Pyrophobia

Searing my young flesh,
a brazen flame hazes the calls of my name.
I feel hell's heat nearing.
With its demons peering,
I kick at the door, I couldn't muster more.
Sheering pain, embodied by the flame.

Then came the blood curdling screams,

my own skin, made into nothing by fire's sin.

Teams of firemen enter.
Schemes forged by the darkest heart,
I'm saved, but the flame is forever the same.
All is destroyed by what the fire deems,

the Devil prefers fire for a reason it seems.

Love's Distain

A touch,
once full of *pleasure*
and *sweet endless time*,
[[[now]]] resembles touch full
of **fish guts** and **slime**.

I'm no longer fooled
          by such ^angled^   flattery,

not after I've suffered,
your   battery.
        misguided

I once *dreamed*
of a future with you.
[[[Now]]] I muster my strength
to – amp | u | tate – love's glue.

My resentful heart
          questions love's intent,
          questions what led me here,
          questions the time I've spent.

What am I to do

                                        in this future

without you…?

The only place
such an answer lies:

                    is within the **thick**
              muck of the Menomin's blue.

The Sculptor's Dilemma

Chisel away at the

It's what we all came in as anyhow.
Show how those years have **withered**
and forged the **structure** yet to be revealed.

Take years into your grasp
and cast away those **POR TION S**
that needed to   *fall off,*
stifling the elusive real
below.

For the archetype must
be in t/ here .
                              somewhere,

hidden in the   plain block.

Make sure that stone image stands,
because what we create
must remain **permanent**
in a world of imper[man]ence.

Chisel away,
because things as they are
                              never stay.
Though the times bring a better day,
 even this
to the
sculpting's   *will*
decay.

Celestial Sailor

A l u m p in the throat.
Sweaty palms and a ricket y boat.
Thrashing winds and a poor raincoat.
What could be keeping this vessel afloat?

Red strained face with despairing eyes.
I feel the boat demolishing, everything d i e s.
          Control is _____ but time
          Let go, everything is in disguise.

The current accepts my shape
and covers my entirety.
The water is calm, the land is what bares
r e l e n t l e s s   a n x i e t y.
Those above the surface bicker about
u n r e a c h a b l e   p r o p r i e t y.
While I find myself in bliss
within this *liquid society.*

I feel again the f e e l i n g I had prior.
Why will this p h e n o m e n o n never retire?
Every day I must **ACT** in this choir.
WHAT FOR? I inquire.
What more would I desire?
While the currents further t r a n s p i r e,
I become what it means to be dire.
I become what flickers the fire.

.
s
e
i
l
f

lost

Identical Difference

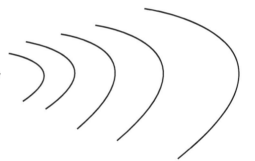

forerunner's

Resonation with frequencies
that filled the atmosphere,
[unseen] but surely heard,

many moons before I

was crawling under the very same Sun. ●

Taking in the tunes of the past's

future testaments.

Speaking of their
modern score,
I [[[now]]] listen
in on what my

_____

expressed with
contemporary vigor.

Let these vibrations
carry the heart's expression,
let it carry further
then that unique
moment, in which,
it was genuinely given.

Let these
shadows casted by
former glories

bring light to our [p[a[r[t[i[a[l]]]]]]]
images of former days under

the very same Sun.

Part 3:
The Underpinnings

"I must know"
I walk up to an ancient tree.
I ask it, "How do you do what you do?"
"I don't know."   "When did you begin?"
"I imagine   right after I ended."
"What   are you exactly?"
"Whatever you want."
Only man will claim
he knows, while his
blood freely distributes
and his world is forever
fluctuating without lead.
Only man can answer
man's questions.
Nature can continue
with its delegated
authority.
So let me
as a man
know who I am,
my purpose,
my hidden fissures.

Until I realize
I fool myself again.
Then I too must say
"I don't know."

The [Forgotten] Talisman

Captivating jazz.
The mahogany slabs creek
under the step of bleak
unknowable consumers.

An unshaven
misbehaving man enters
a respected diner.

He pleads for a simple meal
but he lacks proper parchment.
As **authority**
looms over the clerk,
he forcibly denies his withering guest.

The melody continues,
taking cares away from possessing players.

The dirt-faced man,
happens to be sorely

misplaced,

and is sent back to the same merciless streets
that brought him to such a pitifully
perceived
position.

The forgotten talisman bares
a unique tune, a voice most [unheard].

Yet he dissipates into the cold stone streets
made solely for those who possess
and who are possessed by;
a gregarious greed.

Empty stomached but **whole-heartedly,**

                                    em
                                    an
emancipated but   ci

                                    at
the waste of this country   ed,
embraces his inevitable death
pleased to no longer take in polluted breath.

Maybe:
        a world awaits him
        that recognizes
        this intricate collective sin.

        a world awaits him
        that understands
        the turmoil shared by all.

        a world awaits him
        that won't leave him
        to take most uncertain path
                                    alone.

Yet the jazz keeps playing,
the children learn to
keep their eyes averted.

The slabs still creek
the people don't speak
and they all remain
so dreadfully bleak.

The Bowssening

We, **the holiest** that men can be
Decree that this
rational minded fellow
ought to bellow
all of his **misdeed**.
Then, and only then
will he be freed.

His lack of cooperation
surely leads to his indignation.
Let us **emancipate** him from
that of which, he is.

      Knock him
Nearly drown him   *down*.
in our fictitious liquid.
Quick now, get him to **the steeple**.
That way he can be **surmounted**
by all of **our chosen people**.

Because those that he calls "you"
makes up the things he ought to do
and if we no longer call him mad
then we can quell **the insecurities** we've had.

Until the day that comes
in which, we need to
nearly drown by
the **FORCIBLE** hand.

The church's personal reprimand
against reality as it stand,
tragically gasping within
fictitious liquid.

The Pyrrhus & The Brahman

Even if he is facing d e a t h,

he is   c   h   n   i
               a   g   n
                          g .

With his mass
amount of imagined
opportunity,
he suppresses death.
This wins Pyrrhic victory.
He loses,
yet calls himself a victor.

The newly named **Pyrrhus**
goes through the monotony
                    Passing
of   hour glass lengths.
This has him inquire as to
why he s u f f e r s so.
He finally wonders of
what   lies.
         under

He walks into a [forgotten] old sanctuary.
The floor strewn with [[[[[eternal]]]]] sands.
Within dwells the *Brahman*,
a man of   elusiveness.
Rotten floorboards withstand
The **weight** of his lotus stance.

"Why do you dwell here?"

Why do I dwell?

"Who was I in my last life?"

Who is it that asks?

His dark rooms will remain so
because all great ideas
need to be nourished with the sands.

"Can you tell me who I am?"

*If you wish to know,
stop pretending.*

**"Can you help me come to know
who I am?"**

*Who were you before you
were given name?
What were you before any
of the sharp edges of words
were carved upon you?
What is it that   lies
                      under
all of your
triumphs and sorrows?*

It is I.

The Sage Among the Ten Columned Stage

A sage once told me,
>to let the earth quake,
>to let the wind blow,
>to let go to water's flow
>and let the fire's glow take you.

One cannot squelch the elements.

>What could I be
>besides the fire that
>fluxes within me?

>My feet scathe stone,
>my blood streams.
>This beauty can't be shown
>my world is as he deems.

For this the sage is sought
>and for years I have fought
>to find the wisdom among
>the gloomy mists
>of the ever-growing mountain.

>My tendons burn,
>my throat parched.
>With intent to learn,
>up the expanding mountain I marched.

>Here my eyes meet
>a stage upon ten columns.
>These columns were forged by man

but the scapegoat is God.

>Across the divine sod,
>the stage covers wide span.
>Here many stand, few know why.
>They feel incomplete
>among forged floor

> they believed in the sky.

I feel this hinders them
from their rewarding climb.
But who am I to say?
A product of passing time.

Atop this stage they believed
the sage to be of the Devil.
For if he was not,
would he try to convince you otherwise?
Convoluted logic and
fearful recognitions
led to the sage's end,
lacking of [[[present]]] mortician.

They choked him of breath
drowned him in death,
lit him ablaze,
and buried him under the horizon's glaze.

Being without his elements,
he lies within the divine's sod.
He's now being shamed
like the Lord, God.

I curse the ten fingers
of every man who had hand
in building the ten columns of which
this artificial stage stand.
Men and their false grounds
build expansive towers
just to believe he carries
the more sacred of powers.

I go to the people,
they bare empty eyes.
I tell them the structure
is built on lies.
I try to escape
but the columns are forever built higher.

I feel a deep evil
behind what has forever transpired.
The base starts to tremble.
Earth's plates start to dissemble.
This is when I become
finally apart of…

I stop clinging.
The earth moves,
the wind blows,
I'm consumed by
the water's flows
and at last I feel
what the cosmos knows.

Contingent Linguistics

I speak of the word that is "word."
How absurd it is to say, what it is to say.
For the word is a word, a sound of a sound.
Something we believe to be profound.

But if I don't play
by the rules we use to say,
then the claimed isn't readily
under [display]…

What meaning is there to speak
about that, that is itself.
All description, rendered bleak.
A solid structure of language,
oh look there, a leak. .   .

It boils down to an utterance.
A vibration of sorts.
A message in the air   .
that our mind contorts.

                              .

That which is behind the eye,
ascribes the meaning to be.   .
The one person I will never see.
The absurd word forwarder.
The knower, that is me.   .

Part 4:
The Remnants

the waves said to the rock said to the mind said to the wind said to the waves

An uneasy wind wisps in from the north   A kind whisper travels alongside

With it comes a strange promise

The warm touch of love and the neglect of uncertainty   It sheds the leaves that reflect the misdeeds of summer

We breathe in the circumstances and strive to make it gold

The trees flutter recoiling from the knowing force   The parched grass follows suit. The odd feel its message

The times pass by like the passing glance of a stranger's eye

Each grain feels each collision

No matter how mighty, no matter how miniscule

The waves fold in, but inevitably crash into the sands

The moon lingers above, perfectly positioned, allowing the waves to play their game

I sit on the fringe, witnessing their game, wondering if I am one in the same

If I am but a wave upon the shore, but what more could I ask for?

THE BEDROCK HUMS A DEEP RESONANCE. THIS NEVER MEETS MY EARS BUT EVEN THIS TRANCENDENT TONE IS SUSEPTABLE TO IMPERMANANCE

EVEN THE STRUCTURE THAT HOLDS THE WORLD IN PLACE HAS GAPS IN ITS COMPOSITION NO MATTER THE SOLIDITY

OUR HIGHEST IDEALS AND UTOPIAN APPEALS GIVE WAY TO THE IMPERATIVE DECAY THAT WE SEE EVERYDAY

Cosmic Auditorium

Welcome to the Auditorium.
Inside the acoustics are finely tuned.
The stage is set and the act goes on.

Actors embody the stage
conjure laughter,
contrive tears,
capture fear
cast an illusion,
corporealize meaning.

We act on the world
which acts on itself.
We can't avoid a part;
or the implications.

I need some of this.
I want some of that.
In all these ways
I'm convinced
by the drama
of my act.

The show
never ends.
I am scarcely not
fooled by cosmic actor.

I have never done
anything but
taken part
in this
play.

My Majesty's Magenta Dress

ABOVE.

The heavens particular state,
sees me yearn for her tedious love.
Orders sent down

                                   from the authorities

I render that rebellion is required.
Out casting ————————————————————— myself,
dying to not be
one in the same.

I defy you stars.
Give me life just to say
what I am, where to go, and how to play.

I want what you offer
but don't trust the way
the game has been rigged

                          Passing

within each   day.

The Cosmos, Sun, and Moon
whisper a determined tune
that sounds something like,

       "Solace will come too soon… not soon enough."

But men fight wars and
collect blood soaked currency
to be in arms like hers,
this I know with **CERTAINTY**.

48

My Majesty's magenta dress
strays softly as she steps.
No ill aims needed to find such a beauty.
I fear I may have just found it, here.

Bound by her nearest whim,
I'll stand nearer,
waiting to hear her soothing sound,
whispering words
all the more clearer.

She pushes my hand
where she pleases me to be,
my sought after slavery.   do
                                               w
                                                 n

Just as many fear, I know
that if I allow all of myself to be swept   a   w   a   y ,
little of me may stay,
but this is what I seek.

This is what would keep me ailing
on such dire nights.
This is what would force tears,
when they were not her.
This is what I will [[[[[forever]]]]] yearn for.

So I let myself go,
straying softly as she steps…

deep,

49

Unchanging Vortex

Depth bound probing roots

m ^{e} a ^{n} d ^{e} r

for thick sentiment's
sustaining grasp.

What of me that is
above the surface
withstands the relentless flurries
that carries the seed of my foreign kin.
What ails me prevails another.
The cracking of the sky thunders,
This sends no fear into me,
I am as this world will ever be.

A swirl, an extended circle,
blooms from [nothingness].
Conjured into being
by [unrecognized] forces
at play.
It hurls and twirls,
cascading untethered.

Taking what it wishes
taking my roots from bondage,
taking the bedrock that
was so dearly within
my dependent,
unyielding grasp.
The forces at play would have me
no longer within the fixation
that *nurtured* yet [[[CONFINED]]].

The vortex takes what it wishes
but leaves
as it came,
with [nothing]…

I am left with the ruin,
that of which I have become.
Severed, beaten in a land
I've never known.

Depth bound probing roots

m ^{e} a ^{n} d ^{e} r

for thick sentiment's
sustaining grasp.

Made in the USA
San Bernardino, CA
11 June 2016